W9-BDG-453

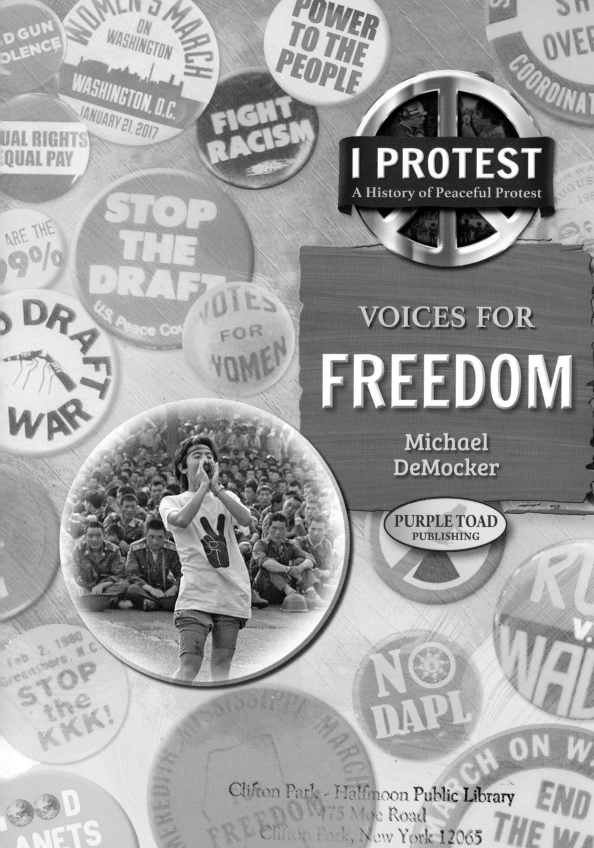

I PROTEST
A History of Peaceful Protest

VOICES FOR
FREEDOM

Michael DeMocker

PURPLE TOAD
PUBLISHING

Printing   1   2   3   4   5   6   7   8   9

Voices for Civil Rights
by Wayne L. Wilson

Voices for the Environment
by Tamra B. Orr

Voices for Equality
by Tamra B. Orr

Voices for Freedom
by Michael DeMocker

Voices for Peace
by Wayne L. Wilson

ABOUT THE AUTHOR
Michael DeMocker is an award-winning author and photojournalist who lives in New Orleans with his wife who is smarter than he is, a son who is taller than he is, and two pugs who mostly ignore him except at meal time.

Publisher's Cataloging-in-Publication Data
DeMocker, Michael.
    Voices for freedom / written by Michael DeMocker.
        p. cm.
Includes bibliographic references, glossary, and index.
ISBN 9781624693717
1. Passive resistance—History—Juvenile literature. 2. Civil disobedience—Juvenile literature. 3. Social action—Juvenile literature. 4. Freedom of speech—Juvenile literature. I. Series: I protest.
    JC328 2017
    323.443

Library of Congress Control Number: 2017940649

ebook ISBN: 9781624693724

CONTENTS

CHAPTER 1
Early
Rumblings

It begins just after dawn. A small group of people, men and women, young and old, gather in the chilly city square by the statue of a despised leader. People carry drums and beat them as they march. One man plays a trumpet. Many marchers carry the flags of their nation. Banging their drums, waving their flags, and holding up their signs and banners, the group marches through the city as it wakes. As the marchers pass by, more people pour from homes or offices to join them. Shopkeepers close their stores and fall in line. They sing patriotic songs and hold their fists in the air in defiance. By the time the marchers reach the presidential palace, the small group has grown to thousands of people. They fill every available space, chanting, singing, and shouting. With one voice they peacefully but forcefully demand that the leader return to them their most precious possession and right: freedom.

This scene and many like it have played out in cities and towns all over the world and at different points in history. Whether demanding their freedom from an oppressive government or an imperial power, history is full of moments

May 30, 1989: The *Goddess of Democracy* rises above protesters in Beijing's Tiananmen Square.

when the common people gather peacefully but in powerful numbers to win back their freedom.

Secession of the Plebeians of Rome

The old Romans all wished to have a king over them because they had not yet tasted the sweetness of freedom.—Titus Livius[1]

In ancient Rome, the citizens were divided into two classes, the patricians and the plebeians, or "plebs." The patricians were the wealthy rulers of Rome who commanded the army and made all the political, legal, and religious decisions. The plebeians were the common folk. They did most of the actual fighting in the wars and had no say in the decisions of the patricians. Plebeians were not allowed to marry patricians. Plebs could not join the patrician class.

Men from the patrician class held all the power. While the plebeians did all the fighting, the patricians reaped the spoils of war. If a pleb fell too far into debt, moneylenders could beat or enslave him. The writer Livy reported that one pleb protester said, "Why don't you pass a law to stop a plebeian from living next door to a patrician, or walking down the same street, or going to the same party, or standing side by side in the Forum?"[2]

Since the plebs could not question the government's decisions, and since the plebs had no voice in the Senate, the plebs had no power in the affairs of the empire. The tension between the plebeians and the patricians came to be called the Conflict of the Orders.

Finally, around 494 BCE, the plebs had had enough. They decided on a protest that was both clever and effective.

They left Rome.

Their protest was called the secession of the plebeians. The plebs closed their shops, walked away from their jobs, and gathered on the Mons Sacre, a hill three miles outside the city. There they stayed, leaving the patricians alone to fend for themselves.

The secession of Rome's plebeians to Mons Sacre as envisioned in an 1849 engraving by B. Barloccini.

The secession convinced the patricians to allow official pleb representatives in government. They were called the "tribunes of the people." The new government was considering a set of laws that would protect all the free citizens of Rome. The plebeians had to leave Rome in protest a *second* time to get the laws adopted. Called the Twelve Tables, these laws were enacted around 449 BCE.

The plebeians would leave Rome in protest at least three more times— in 445 BCE, 342 BCE, and finally in 287 BCE. The last time, the protest forced

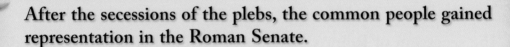

After the secessions of the plebs, the common people gained representation in the Roman Senate.

the patricians to adopt the *Lex Hortensia*, a law that gave plebeians the right to pass laws that had to be obeyed by all Roman citizens (even the patricians). This law brought an the end to the Conflict of Orders.

It took over two centuries and many nonviolent protest marches out of Rome, but finally, the plebs had the freedom to govern alongside the patricians.

BREAD AND CIRCUSES

During the secession of the plebs, Rome was a Republic. The country had overthrown the monarchy and established a government whose ruling class—the patricians—elected leaders to represent them. Each year, they elected two consuls, who ruled as a king would rule. A senate made the laws of the land.

The Roman Republic gave way to the Roman Empire. Its strong military helped Rome spread

A chariot race

throughout the Mediterranean area. Though the plebs were now represented in the Senate, they were increasingly poor. To keep them happy, Emperor Augustus (reigned 31 BCE – 14 CE) started a program of free grain to keep people fed. He also offered free entertainment—gladiator games, chariot races, and other spectacles. The writer Juvenal called these distractions "bread and circuses."

The term "bread and circuses" is still used to describe methods of distracting the public from important issues in their lives. Whether it be the newest comedy series on television, the most extreme video game, or the latest sports championship held in a modern arena, distractions keep people happy. In times of great unrest, however, citizens will look past these entertainments and stand up for their homes, families, and fellow human beings.

CHAPTER 2
Tea and Salt

Boston Tea Party

It does not take a majority to prevail ... but rather an irate, tireless minority, keen on setting brushfires of freedom in the minds of men.—Samuel Adams[1]

The United States of America began life as a collection of British colonies. The English king and his government ruled these colonies from across the Atlantic Ocean. Before long, the colonists wanted freedom and independence from the king.

On March 22, 1765, the British Parliament passed the Stamp Act. The colonists had to pay a tax in the form of a stamp on any piece of paper or document they used. All the money from the tax went right to the British government. The colonists called this "taxation without representation," because they had no one to speak up for them if they felt they were being treated unfairly.

To make things worse, on May 10, 1773, the British Parliament passed the Tax Act, which favored Britain's East

Colonists protest the Stamp Act, which said they had to pay the British government a tax in the form of a stamp on any piece of paper or document they used.

A 1774 political cartoon from *London Magazine* shows a Native American, symbol of the colonies, swallowing a "bitter draught"—in this case, the Intolerable Acts.

India Company. The Tax Act refunded the tax the company paid on tea. Colonial merchants did not get the same break, so their tea cost more than the tea from the East India Company. The colonists knew this was unfair. They decided to take their anger out on imported tea.

On September 27, seven tea ships set out from England bound for the colonies. When the *Nancy* arrived in New York City, a large group of protesters met her at the dock. They made the ship turn back for home with its cargo of tea. The *Polly* had the same experience in Philadelphia. A third ship, the *London*, docked in Charleston, South Carolina. Rebellious colonists seized its cargo of tea. Another ship, the *William*, never made it to harbor. It was shipwrecked in a storm.

The three remaining tea ships—the *Dartmouth*, the *Eleanor*, and the *Beaver*—made it into Boston Harbor and docked at Griffin's Wharf. The leaders of the resistance to British rule—the Patriots—decided that the tea should never make it to land.

On the cold, foggy night of December 16, 1773, over one hundred protesters, calling themselves the Sons of Liberty, sneaked aboard the three ships. Many were disguised as Native Americans to show their preference for America over Britain.[2] They crept belowdecks and hauled up heavy lead-lined crates of tea. The protesters spent the next three hours bashing open the crates with axes and dumping the tea into the water. Scores of spectators watched from shore.

December 16, 1773: Cheered by supporters on the docks, over a hundred protesters calling themselves the Sons of Liberty raid British tea ships docked in Boston Harbor.

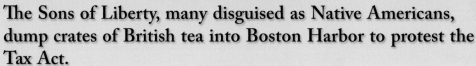

The Sons of Liberty, many disguised as Native Americans, dump crates of British tea into Boston Harbor to protest the Tax Act.

By the time the raiders had finished, 340 crates filled with a total of 90,000 pounds of tea were dumped into Boston Harbor. At today's prices, that was over $1 million worth of tea.[3] When it was over, no member of the tea ships' crews was harmed, the ships were not damaged, and there was no violence between the protesters and the British troops stationed in Boston. Boston Harbor, however, smelled of tea for weeks to come.

King George III and the British Parliament were not pleased about the Boston Tea Party. In March 1774, the British government imposed the Intolerable Acts upon the colonies. These new rules included closing the port of Boston and stripping the state of Massachusetts of its governing powers. Rather than putting down the rebellion, the Intolerable Acts only united the colonies in their quest for freedom. War broke out, and the fledging colonists eventually won their independence from England.

Gandhi and the Salt Marches

When I despair, I remember that all through history the way of truth and love has always won. There have been tyrants and murderers and for a time they seem invincible, but in the end, they always fall—think of it, always.

—Mahatma Gandhi[4]

Since the middle of the nineteenth century, India had been a colony of the British Empire. The people of India believed British imperialism robbed them of their freedom. A Hindu lawyer, Mohandas Karamchand Gandhi, led the movement to free India from British control. Gandhi was from the western town of Gujarat. Educated in London, he worked for civil rights by helping Indians in South Africa. When he returned in 1915, he helped fight to free India from British rule. Gandhi began a campaign of nonviolent but forceful resistance called *satyagraha*, based on the Sanskrit words *satya*, meaning "truth," and *agraha*, meaning "firmness."[5]

The British Empire claimed the rights to salt production

Hindu lawyer Mohandas Karamchand Gandhi sought to free India from British rule.

15

The British Empire removed huge amounts of resources from India, further impoverishing the already struggling citizens of the country.

in India. The people of India could not sell or collect salt for their own use. They had to buy the salt from the British, and the British taxed it heavily. Salt was important to the health of the people of India. It was vital to replace the salt lost to sweat while working in the hot climate. Having a ruling power from across the seas control this basic and essential mineral angered the people of India.

The British oppressed the people of India in many ways, but Gandhi saw the salt tax as a cause that the people could fight. On March 12, 1930, Gandhi and seventy-eight of his followers left his base near Gujarat and began a 240-mile march to the town of Dandi by the Arabian Sea. There, they would collect salt in violation of British law.

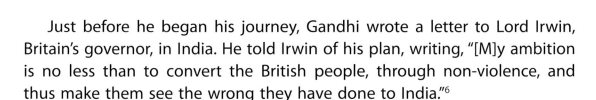

Just before he began his journey, Gandhi wrote a letter to Lord Irwin, Britain's governor, in India. He told Irwin of his plan, writing, "[M]y ambition is no less than to convert the British people, through non-violence, and thus make them see the wrong they have done to India."[6]

Wearing a pair of sandals and carrying a walking stick, Gandhi led his group of protesters. They covered about a dozen miles a day. Along the way, they would stop at towns and Gandhi would give speeches. He would ask the town leaders to quit in protest, and for people to join him on the march. Twenty-four days later—on April 5, followed by a column of tens of thousands of protesters that stretched for many miles—Gandhi arrived at the seashore where salt was plentiful. There, he defied the Salt Act by

March 12, 1930: Gandhi and seventy-eight of his followers left Gujarat and began a 240-mile "salt march" to the town of Dandi by the Arabian Sea.

reaching down and collecting a handful of salt. He said, "With this, I am shaking the foundations of the British Empire."[7]

After this simple and symbolic act, millions of people protested all across India. They organized more salt marches. They boycotted British stores. An estimated 80,000 people, including Gandhi himself, were jailed during these protests.[8]

Gandhi once said of fighting for change, "First they ignore you, then they laugh at you, then they fight you, then you win." After being released from jail in January of 1931, Gandhi met with Lord Irwin. They agreed that Gandhi would call off the boycotts and protests against the British. In return, thousands of political prisoners would be released, the British Salt Act would be repealed, and, most importantly, the people of India would have a voice in their future. While the struggle for freedom continued for many years, Gandhi's Salt March helped pave the way for India's eventual independence from British rule in 1947.

April 5, 1930: Gandhi defies the Salt Act by collecting a handful of salt from the seashore, saying, "With this, I am shaking the foundations of the British Empire."

McCarthy and the Green Feather Movement

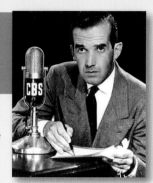

Edward R. Murrow

Nearly two hundred years after the United States gained independence, the country faced another type of oppression in the 1950s. Afraid of a Russian takeover, the U.S. government cracked down on political freedom. Led by Senator Joseph McCarthy and the House Un-American Activities Committee (HUAC), Congress and law enforcement officers targeted people they believed were promoting communism. (Communism is the form of government practiced by the Russians.) They questioned hundreds of people, hoping to cleanse the United States of communist ideas. People from all walks of life—from teachers to Hollywood movie stars, artists, and writers—were accused of being traitors. They were blacklisted—companies were secretly told not to hire them. They were also pressured to name more "traitors."

In 1953, an Indiana textbook official wanted to ban the book *Robin Hood* from schools. The book, she said, promoted communism because Robin Hood stole from the rich and gave to the poor. Students at the University of Indiana protested. They passed around green feathers like the one in Robin Hood's hat. Soon, students across the nation were joining the Green Feather Movement. They encouraged writing to members of congress to oppose McCarthyism.

In 1954, respected journalist Edward R. Murrow attacked McCarthy and his methods on television's *See It Now*. Murrow urged Americans to "not confuse dissent with disloyalty."[9] It had an impact. Public approval started to turn against McCarthy. He angered more people when he began investigating U.S. Army personnel for communist activities.

Later that year, Democrats took control of Congress. The Senate soon reprimanded McCarthy for his actions. His witch hunts at last began to end.

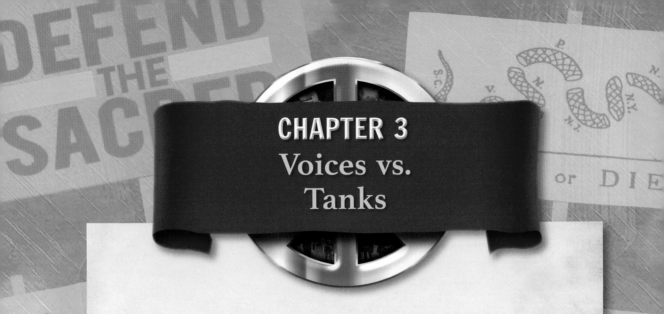

People Power Revolution

I'll never wash this hand. It pushed back a tank.

—Protester in Manila, February 23, 1986[1]

Ferdinand Marcos was elected president of the Philippines in 1965. In 1972, he declared martial law, then imprisoned or banished his opposition. He stayed in power long after his term as president ended. Marcos became a dictator.

One of his most vocal opponents was Ninoy Aquino, Jr. When Aquino returned from the United States in 1983, he was assassinated at the Manila airport. The murder caused a great outcry. In order to calm the people, Marcos ordered an early, or "snap," election in February 1986. Aquino's widow, Corazon, or Cory, ran against Marcos, but Marcos was declared the winner. Many people believed the vote was rigged in the dictator's favor. Dozens of computer technicians in charge of counting the ballot walked out in protest. They believed the election results were being changed to reelect Marcos.[2]

December 30, 1969: Ferdinand Marcos is sworn in for his second presidential term in Manila. Many people in the Philippines believe the election was tampered with.

Cory Aquino

Aquino declared herself to be the true winner of the election. On February 16, she addressed a crowd of two million people in Manila, calling for a campaign of civil disobedience against the government called "Triumph of the People."[3] She asked the people to skip paying their utility bills to the government and to avoid buying anything from government-owned businesses. Cardinal Ricardo Vidal called for the people to reject the rigged election. In a letter to his church members, he wrote, "If such a government does not of itself freely correct the evil it has inflicted on the people then it is our serious moral obligation as a people to make it do so."[4]

High-ranking members of the military joined the voices calling for Marcos to step down. Their first attempt at a coup failed, but other military defections soon followed.

Beginning on February 22, hundreds of thousands of protesters gathered on Manila's Epifanio de los Santos Avenue, or EDSA, to call for Marcos to step down. Many wore yellow clothing or sported yellow ribbons, giving the protest the nickname "The Yellow Revolution." Protesters held up their fingers as an L, meaning *laban*, or "fight."

Radio Veritas, a non-government radio station broadcasting from a building owned by the Catholic Church, called on citizens to join the protesters and to help protect them from the pro-Marcos forces. After their transmitter was destroyed by soldiers early on February 23, they switched to a smaller back-up transmitter and continued to broadcast their anti-Marcos messages.[5]

Later in the day, a line of tanks approached the protesters. Tens of thousands of people blocked them, including nuns who prayed the rosary and held up crosses. A wheelchair-bound elderly woman holding a crucifix begged the tanks not to kill the young people. A soldier got down from his

Corazon Aquino became the new Filipino president after Marcos fled the country on February 25, 1986.

tank and hugged her as the people cheered.[6] The tanks left without firing a shot.

On Monday, February 24, helicopters and gunships from the Philippines Air Force swooped down and landed near an estimated two million protesters. Instead of attacking, they turned their guns around to protect the gathering. By the end of the protests, about 80 percent of the military had switched sides.[7]

On February 25, under pressure from the citizens, the church, and the military, the powerless Ferdinand Marcos and his family fled the presidential palace. Corazon Aquino was sworn in as the new Filipino president on the same day. Filipinos took to the street in celebration of their freedom in the "Bloodless Revolution."

The Singing Revolution
Ükskord me võidame niikuinii! (One day, no matter what, we will win!)
—Estonian activist Heinz Valk[8]

In 1939, Estonia and its Baltic neighbors Lithuania and Latvia were seized by the USSR (the Union of Soviet Socialist Republics, or Soviet Union). In Estonia, it was illegal to sing patriotic songs or fly the Estonian flag. For the next fifty years, Estonia and its neighbors were ruled by Moscow, the capital of the Soviet Union. They were unable to chart their own course or celebrate their own history.

As the Soviet Union began to weaken in the late 1980s, Estonians demonstrated for independence. They fought for freedom not with weapons, but with song. On May 14, 1988, concertgoers at the Tartu Pop Music Festival showed up waving Estonian flags. Led by the musicians on stage, they sang banned patriotic songs in protest. The "Singing Revolution" had begun, as musicians and concertgoers all over the country sang in protest.

This was not the first time the Estonians used song as an act of resistance. They had sung against German invaders in the thirteenth century and again against the Russian czar and his army in the eighteenth century.[9]

On September 11, 1988, more than 300,000 people, a quarter of the Estonian population, crowded into the "Song of Estonia" music festival.[10] In the open-air Tallinn Song Festival Grounds, they sang banned songs and listened to political speakers demand independence from the Soviet Union.

The highlight of this fight for freedom came on August 23, 1989, on the fiftieth anniversary of Soviet rule. That evening, over two million Estonians, Latvians, and Lithuanians joined hands to form a human chain.[11] It stretched down the roads and over the farms of all three countries. In Estonia, the password to join the "Baltic Chain" was "freedom."[12] One participant described the chain like this: "The Berlin Wall is made of brick and concrete. Our wall is stronger."[13] Throughout the evening, the people sang patriotic songs, held candles, waved national flags, and demanded their independence. Twenty-five years later, U.S. President Barack Obama called this protest "one of the greatest displays of freedom and nonviolent resistance that the world has ever seen."[14]

In August 1991, Soviet tanks rolled across the border into Estonia to discourage further revolt, but it was too late. Estonians faced down the tanks and rushed to protect radio and TV stations from being taken over. Within a matter of weeks, Estonia and its neighbors were officially recognized by their former Soviet masters as independent and free countries.

The Baltic Chain stretched across three countries.

Dictatorships

Although Ferdinand Marcos was democratically elected, he became a dictator through fraud (lying) and force. Other dictators have come into power using similar tactics. In a dictatorship, one person or a small group of people governs. Dictators are usually not limited by a constitution, and they cannot be replaced through elections. In dictatorships, citizens are generally powerless—until, that is, they unite.

Srdja Popovic and Slobodan Djinovic have plenty of experience in organizing nonviolent protests against dictators. They led the organization Otpor, a group that helped overthrow dictator Slobodan Milosevic in Serbia in 2000. The two then went on to help democracy movements in Ukraine and Georgia. By 2015, they had founded the Center for Applied Nonviolent Action and Strategies (Canvas) and trained activists in 46 countries.

In Syria in 2011, a small group of people met with Popovic and Djinovic to figure out how to oust President Bashar al-Assad. They planned their strategies carefully, and gained widespread support. Many other nonviolent resisters organize separate groups. Some of these groups turned violent. Assad arrested, killed, or deported nonviolent leaders, weakening the movement. At the same time, he released known terrorists from jail to work for him. Civil war broke out.

Bashar al-Assad

Many believe that nonviolence failed in Syria, but the groups have not given up. Nonviolent resisters have continued to organize. They lead peace circles, report on Assad's crimes against the people, provide education and healing for children, and plan for a stronger civilian base once the war is over.

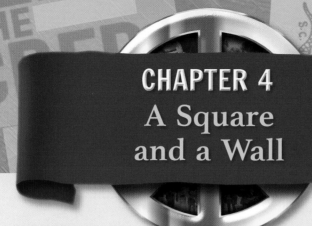

CHAPTER 4
A Square and a Wall

Tiananmen Square

The packed square became the city's pulsing heart; the police had vanished. This was a benevolent form of anarchy—noble, joyous, and surprisingly orderly.

—Author Ma Jian on the scene in Tiananmen Square, 1989[1]

China is a communist country in Asia. Its government bans free expression and controls the media. It does not allow free elections to its most important offices. Hu Yaobang, a former party general secretary, was considered very open-minded to changing China to a democracy. On April 15, 1989, he died suddenly of a heart attack. Students hoping for more freedoms were greatly upset.[2] In the following week, over one hundred thousand students gathered in Tiananmen Square ("Gate of Heavenly Peace") to demand freedom of speech, democratic elections, and an end to corruption. The protests spread to college campuses across China.

On May 1, thousands of protesting students began a hunger strike, refusing food and camping atop parked buses. A few days after the hunger strikes began, workers drove a parade of motorcycles through the streets in support of the

Hundreds of thousands of protesters filled Beijing's Tiananmen Square in May of 1989 to demand democratic reforms.

protesters. By May 17, the protesters in Beijing numbered more than one million people.[3] In the days that followed, the hunger strikes began to take their toll. Over 8,000 protesters were hospitalized.[4]

University professors arrived in large numbers on May 20 to join their students. That same day, the Chinese government declared martial law and sent soldiers to end the demonstration. Civilians blocked their trucks, and the soldiers eventually turned back.

On May 29, art students from the Central Academy of Fine Arts built a 37-foot-high statue using paper-mache and foam. They called it *The Goddess of Democracy*. The statue reawakened the protest, drawing hundreds of thousands of people to the square just to see her.

On June 1, the Chinese government stopped all foreign media from reporting in Tiananmen Square. Early in the morning of June 4, tanks and soldiers were ordered to end the protest. Fifty trucks and an estimated 10,000 soldiers entered the square.[5]

Art students from the Central Academy of Fine Arts build a 37-foot-high statue in Tiananmen Square called *The Goddess of Democracy*.

The troops opened fire on the unarmed protesters. No one knows for sure how many were killed in the violent suppression of the protest. The Chinese government says 241 people died, but other estimates are as high as 7,000.[6] As many as 10,000 protesters were arrested.[7] A tank crushed *The Goddess of Democracy*.[8]

The protesters would have one last moment. The day after the massacre, an unknown man was photographed standing in front of a line of tanks, stopping them. This is now one of the most famous images of the twentieth century. It is forbidden to show the picture of "The Tank Man" in China.

Today, the Chinese government bans all mention of the events of 1989. History books make no mention of the protests and massacre, and you can't search the Internet in China for stories about what happened.

In China, you would not be allowed to read this book.

"The Tank Man" stands in front of a column of tanks after the violent government suppression of protesters in Tiananmen Square.

The Berlin Wall

It's always the small people who change things. It's never the politicians or the big guys. I mean, who pulled down the Berlin wall? It was all the people in the streets.—Movie director Luc Besson[9]

After World War II, the victorious Allies—the United States, France, the Soviet Union, and the United Kingdom—divided the vanquished country of Germany into four "zones of occupation." They also divided the capital of Berlin into four sectors. But after the war, these powerful countries began to battle for power and territory, beginning an era of conflict called the Cold War. A divided Germany became one of the most visible symbols of the Cold War. The eastern part of the country, and of Berlin, was under the control of the Soviet Union. The western parts were under the control of the United States and its allies. People began moving from the east to the west in great numbers.

Early in the morning on Sunday, August 13, 1961, the East's German Democratic Republic built a barbed-wire fence between the eastern half of Berlin and the western half. The day came to be called "Barbed Wire Sunday." Within weeks, a huge concrete wall protected by armed guards and booby traps was built. It was over 85 miles long and had hundreds of watchtowers. Over the next generation, scores of people were killed trying to escape from the east to the west. Many Berliners thought that Germany would never become one again.[10]

In the late 1980s, the Soviet Union began to weaken. Many of the repressive Soviet-backed regimes in East Germany's neighboring countries fell. East Germans began to demand more freedom to travel to the west and called for the borders to be opened. A popular chant at these protests was *"Wir wollen raus!"* or "Let us out!"

On November 4, 1989, actors and theater workers in East Berlin organized a peaceful march at the Alexanderplatz in the center of East Berlin. It drew between half a million and one million protesters.[11] They demanded political

November 4, 1989: Between a half million and one million protesters gather at the Alexanderplatz in the center of East Berlin to demand political reforms, free elections, and freedom to travel to the West.

reform, free elections, and more freedom to travel. The organizers arranged for dozens of parade marshals to wear green and yellow sashes that read, "No Violence."[12]

Authorities in East Germany were facing another crisis. Besides the protesters, a large number of refugees were leaving neighboring Hungary and Czechoslovakia. On November 9, authorities would announce a temporary loosening of restrictions at the border checkpoints. It would go into effect in the coming days.

The spokesman for the ruling party, Günter Schabowski, was holding a press conference that day. He was handed a note about the changes but nothing more. He read the new order but didn't realize it wasn't going into effect until the borders guards were notified. When asked when the new rule took effect, he wrongly said, "Immediately."

People were stunned. The press reported the borders were now free and open, which wasn't true. Around 20,000 people gathered at the checkpoints, demanding to be let past the Berlin Wall.[13] Commanders at the border crossings realized their soldiers were badly outnumbered. Not wanting violence to erupt, they simply pulled their men back and let the people through.

Once on the other side, the East and West Germans celebrated. They danced and drank champagne well into the early hours, many still in their pajamas, despite the chilly night.[14] Revelers from both sides jumped on the Berlin Wall to dance.

In the days that followed, people from both sides began to chip away at the massive wall with tools, opening holes and taking souvenirs. By the following summer, the East German military had begun to tear down the Berlin Wall, and East Germans were given more freedom to travel.

On October 3, 1990, less than a year after the massive nonviolent protest for freedom at Alexanderplatz, Germany was reunified as a single, free country.

Protesters stand atop the Berlin Wall near the Brandenburg Gate as East and West Berliners celebrate.

Communism vs. Socialism

The members of the Soviet Union were considered communist countries. However, the full name of the Soviet Union is the Union of Soviet Socialist Republics (USSR). How could they be both communist and socialist?

The Soviet Union based its political ideas on *The Communist Manifesto*, a book written by Karl Marx and Friedrich Engels. They believed that capitalism—the pursuit of money for personal gain—took advantage of the working class. While it made the rich richer, capitalism was not good for society. The goal, they said, was to have a society without currency, class, or personal property. Everyone would share the goods and services produced by the society as a whole. This goal was called communism.

To reach that goal, the society would first have to practice socialism. Elected representatives would be in charge of production and of the distribution of goods and services. The USSR started as socialist, with the goal of becoming communist.

These concepts seem to make sense. In reality, when representatives choose what is good for society, individual freedoms are lost. Individuals who do not go along with everyone else are seen as dangerous. Freedom of religion, freedom of expression, and owning personal property are not tolerated. Even travel may be restricted, as it was in East Germany.

Karl Marx

To regain these personal freedoms, people around the world have protested. Some of them have succeeded in changing their governments. Others are still fighting.

CHAPTER 5
A Continuing Struggle

Arab Spring, Egypt

Revolution is like a love story. When you are in love, you become a much better person. And when you are in revolution, you become a much better person.

—Egyptian author Alaa Al Aswany[1]

For three decades—1981 to 2011—one man had ruled Egypt: Hosni Mubarak. Egyptians blamed him for the poverty, unemployment, and corruption plaguing the country.[2] They became angry when Mubarak proposed giving power directly to his son Gamal.[3] Emboldened by a revolt in neighboring Tunisia that caused the president to flee the country two weeks earlier, thousands of people decided to protest. They marched through Cairo on January 25, 2011, a national holiday meant to honor the police force. The crowd chanted, "Down with Mubarak."

The march was peaceful at first, but as protesters gathered in the large Tahir ("Liberation") Square, police fired tear gas into the crowd. The first day of protests was called "The Day of Rage."

January 25, 2011: Protesters march to Cairo's Tahir Square to protest the rule of Hosni Mubarak.

A soldier watches the protests in Tahir Square from atop a tank.

Over the next few days, protests continued and grew in Cairo and other Egyptian cities. Thousands of Egyptians attempted to force change through strikes, marches, and demonstrations. They demanded free elections, freedom of speech, and an end to corruption. Social media played a large role in unifying the protesters. The government responded by trying to shut down the country's Internet.

January 28 was dubbed "The Friday of Anger" as hundreds of thousands of protesters descended on Tahir Square. The government was said to have opened the doors of the city's prisons to put criminals on the street to scare the protesters away.[4]

The following day, the government issued a curfew, ordering everyone to go home. Tens of thousands of protesters ignored it. Some protesters even camped out in tents in the square.[5] A new chant became the rallying

cry of the Egyptian protesters: "Lift up your head. You're Egyptian." Over the next couple of days, the crowds in Tahir Square grew to an estimated quarter million people.[6]

February 1 was called "The March of the Millions." More than one million protesters crammed into Tahir Square to demand freedom from Mubarak's oppressive government. The following day, police and pro-Mubarak *baltagiya* ("goons" or "thugs") were accused of riding into Tahir Square on camels and horses taken from the tourist sections of Cairo. What became known as the Battle of the Camels lasted well into the next day. It failed to drive the protesters from the square.[7]

Hundreds of thousands of protesters declared February 4 to be a "Friday of Departure," which they hoped would end with Mubarak leaving office. Instead, he stayed.

Protesters held "The Sunday of the Martyrs" on February 6 as both Christians and Muslims came together to remember those who had died during the previous days of protest. Though the protest was intended to be nonviolent, there were many clashes between police and protesters. Over the course of eighteen days, many people on both sides died, and many more were injured.

On February 8, "The Day of Egypt's Love," the largest crowds yet took to the streets.[8] The following day, widespread

February 4, 2011: Hundreds of thousands of protesters gather for the "Friday of Departure."

strikes were called throughout the country. On February 10, Mubarak appeared on television and said he would not step down. Protesters responded by waving the soles of their shoes in the air, a sign of great disrespect in Arab culture.

The next day was indeed "The Day of Departure." Hundreds of thousands of protesters again took to the streets of cities throughout Egypt. Finally, at 4:00 in the afternoon, Mubarak officially stepped down as president. The wild celebration in Tahir Square continued until dawn the next day. Two months later, Mubarak was arrested for corruption and abuse of office.

The revolutions in Tunisia and Egypt were part of a larger movement called the Arab Spring. People throughout the Middle East in countries such as Libya, Yemen, Saudi Arabia, Jordan, Syria, and Bahrain followed the example of Egypt. They rose up to demand more freedom.

February 11, 2011: Celebrations break out in Tahir Square after Mubarak officially steps down as president.

March 19, 2011: Egyptians line up to vote in Mokattam, Cairo, for a constitutional referendum. More than 18 million people turned out to vote.

While the world has changed greatly since the Conflict of Orders in ancient Rome, one thing has remained constant throughout the ages: citizens will band together to demand freedom from their leaders, whether it be freedom from oppression, freedom from unfair treatment, or freedom from political corruption.

Even today, people take to the streets demanding change. From September to December of 2014, tens of thousands of umbrella-toting residents clogged the streets of Hong Kong. Streets and businesses had to close. Called the "Umbrella Revolution," the people were protesting the Chinese government, which had failed to deliver their promise of free elections in Hong Kong.

In November 2016 in South Korea, over a quarter million people protested in the capital of Seoul. They demanded that President Park Geun-hye be removed from her office for corruption. After many additional protests, she was impeached in March 2017.

March 26, 2017: Thousands of Russians protest in Moscow and throughout the country demanding an end to what they believe is widespread government corruption.

Huge rallies all across Russia on Sunday, March 26, 2017, saw thousands of people demanding an end to what they believe was widespread government corruption. In the capital of Moscow, protesters were confronted by police in riot gear. They responded by shooting videos and selfies with their cell phones and posting them to social media.

On Wednesday, April 19, 2017, citizens of Venezuela held "the Mother of All Protests." Hundreds of thousands of angry people took to the streets to demand the removal of President Nicolas Maduro. Many saw Maduro as becoming increasingly dictatorial as well as responsible for widespread food shortages.

From the *secessio plebis* of ancient Rome to selfies with riot police in downtown Moscow, citizens have found ways to demand changes in their governments in nonviolent ways. Sometimes these protests are successful and sometimes they are not, but one thing is sure: If protesters continue to gather together and speak with one voice, they will be heard.

THE GREEN MOVEMENT

There seemed little doubt. A nation's presidential election had been tampered with. The people did not trust the results, and so they stood together in mass protest against the new president. The time was June, 2009, and the country was Iran.

Mahmoud Ahmadinejad had been declared the victor in the closest presidential election in Iran's history. The people were convinced it had been rigged. On June 25, 2009, a huge rally took place that asked, "Where is my vote?" It was called The Green Movement. Iranians took to the streets with fingers painted green they would hold up to cry out for peace and justice. It was just the beginning of protests that would last until the following year.

Leaders of the movement were arrested, voices were suppressed, and even human rights activists were imprisoned. Although the mass protests stopped, and Ahmadinejad remained president, it remains in the minds and hearts of many Iranians who want a democracy. It still serves as a shining example of non-violent protest for civil rights-minded people all over the world.

Green clothing and ribbons were also worn during the Green Movement protests.

BCE

494 The plebeians of Rome, protesting their treatment by the patricians, abandon the city in the first "secession of the plebs."

449 The Twelve Tables, a new set of laws that gives the plebeians a voice in government, is enacted after a second walk-out.

287 A final secession of the plebs follows similar walk-outs in 445 and 342 BCE. It ends the Conflict of Orders, as all Roman citizens are granted equal protection under the law.

CE

1773 December 16: To protest an unfair tax on tea, over one hundred Sons of Liberty climb aboard three ships in Boston Harbor and dump 90,000 pounds of tea overboard.

1930 March 12: Mohandas Karamchand Gandhi and seventy-eight followers begin a 240-mile march to the town of Dandi by the Arabian Sea to collect salt, protesting the British salt tax.

1950–1954 U.S. Senator Joseph McCarthy targets U.S. citizens who he believes are communists. People protest his witch hunts.

1965 December 30: Ferdinand Marcos becomes president of the Philippines. He soon becomes a dictator.

1983 August 21: Marcos opponent Benigno Aquino Jr. is assassinated at Manila International Airport.

1986 February 22: Hundreds of thousands of protesters, led by Aquino's widow, Corazon, fill Manila's Epifanio de los Santos Avenue. They demand an end to the Marcos dictatorship. Marcos flees the country on February 25.

1988 May 14: Concertgoers at the Tartu Pop Music Festival wave Estonian flags and sing banned songs in protest of the Soviet Union's fifty-year control of the country.

September 11: Over 300,000 people crowd into the "Song of Estonia" music festival to sing banned songs and to listen to political speakers demand independence.

1989 April: After Hu Yaobang, a former party general secretary in China, dies suddenly of a heart attack, more than one hundred thousand students begin to occupy Beijing's Tiananmen Square to demand more freedom. They are hoping for democratic reforms.

May 29: Students from China's Central Academy of Fine Arts build a 37-foot-high statue called *The Goddess of Democracy*.

June 4: Chinese government tanks and soldiers enter Tiananmen Square to end the protest by force. They kill an unknown number of protesters.

August 23: On the fiftieth anniversary of Soviet rule, more than two million Estonians, Latvians, and Lithuanians join hands to form a human chain. It stretches across all three countries.

November 4: On the East Berlin side of the wall, a peaceful demonstration at the Alexanderplatz draws between half a million and one million protesters. They demand political reforms and freedom of travel.

November 9: After an announcement that the restrictions at the Berlin Wall would be loosened, 20,000 people gather at the checkpoints. They demand to be let past the Berlin Wall and eventually rush through. Over the next few days, citizens on both sides begin to dismantle the wall.

1990   October 3: Germany is reunified as a single, free country.

2011   January 25: Thousands of Egyptian protesters gather in Cairo's Tahir Square for a "Day of Rage." They demand that President Hosni Mubarak step down.

February 8: After two weeks of protesting, the largest number of people yet demonstrate on "The Day of Egypt's Love."

February 11: On "The Day of Departure," hundreds of thousands of protesters again protest in cities throughout Egypt. Mubarak steps down as president.

2014   September to December: Tens of thousands of Hong Kong residents shut down the streets and close businesses during the "Umbrella Revolution."

2016   November: Hundreds of thousands of protesters fill the streets of Seoul, South Korea. They demand the removal of President Park Geun-hye for corruption.

2017   March 26: Thousands of Russians demand an end to what they believe is widespread government corruption. They march in the capital of Moscow and other Russian cities.

April 19: Venezuelans hold "the Mother of All Protests" as hundreds of thousands march in Caracas and other cities. They demand the removal of President Nicolas Maduro, whom they see as becoming increasingly dictatorial as well as responsible for widespread food shortages.

Chapter 1. Early Rumblings

1. Livy. *History of Rome, Vol 1., Books 1-2* (Cambridge, MA: Harvard University Press 1919), Book 1, section 17.
2. Beard, Mary. *SPQR* (New York: Liveright Publishing, 2015), p. 147.

Chapter 2. Tea and Salt

1. Baker, Mark Allen. *Spies of Revolutionary Connecticut: From Benedict Arnold to Nathan Hale* (Stroud, UK: The History Press, 2014), p. 47.
2. Boston Tea Party Ship & Museum: "Disguise of Sons of Liberty." www.bostonteapartyship.com/tea-blog/boston-tea-party-disguise
3. The History Channel: "The Boston Tea Party." www.history.com/topics/american-revolution/boston-tea-party
4. Gandhi, Mohandas K. *Gandhi: An Autobiography: The Story of My Experiments with Truth* (Boston: Beacon Press, 1993).
5. Ibid.
6. Ibid.
7. Ibid., p. 240.
8. The History Channel: "Salt March." www.history.com/topics/salt-march
9. Murrow, Edward R. "A Report on Senator Joseph R. McCarthy." *See It Now*, CBS, March 9, 1954. https://www.youtube.com/watch?v=kgejIbN9UYA

Chapter 3. Voices vs. Tanks

1. Nepstad, Sharon Erickson. *Nonviolent Revolutions: Civil Resistance in the Late 20th Century* (Oxford: Oxford University Press, 2011), p. 3.
2. Ibid., p. 118.
3. Ibid.
4. Ibid., p. 182.
5. Reyes-Estrope, Carmela. "Radyo Veritas Role in EDSA I Recalled." *Philippine Daily Inquirer*, February 25, 2015. http://newsinfo.inquirer.net/675077/veritas-role-in-edsa-i-recalled
6. Nepstad, p. 120.
7. Ibid., p. 3.
8. Obama, Barack. "Remarks by President Obama to the People of Estonia." The White House Office of the Press Secretary, September 3, 2014.
9. International Center on Nonviolent Conflict: "Estonia's Singing Revolution (1986–1991)." https://www.nonviolent-conflict.org/estonias-singing-revolution-1986-1991/
10. Ibid.
11. Ibid.
12. Obama.
13. Ibid.
14. Ibid.

Chapter 4. A Square and a Wall

1. Jian, Ma. "The Great Tiananmen Taboo." *The Guardian*, June 1., 2009.
2. Starr, John Bryan. *Understanding China: A Guide to China's Economy, History, and Political Culture* (New York: Hill and Wang, 2010), p. 88.
3. Ibid., p. 90.
4. Nepstad, Sharon Erickson. *Nonviolent Revolutions: Civil Resistance in the Late 20th Century* (Oxford: Oxford University Press, 2011), p. 26.
5. Raymon, Noah. "6 Things You Should Know about the Tiananmen Square Massacre." *TIME*, n. d. www.time.com/2822290/tiananmen-square-massacre-facts-time
6. Starr, p. 90.
7. CNN Library. "Tiananmen Square Fast Facts." CNN, May 28, 2017. www.cnn.com/2013/09/15/world/asia/tiananmen-square-fast-facts
8. Ibid.
9. "Luc Besson: Guardian Interviews at the BFI." *The Guardian*, March 23, 2000. https://www.theguardian.com/film/2000/mar/23/guardianinterviewsatbfisouthbank1
10. Taylor, Frederick. *The Berlin Wall: A World Divided, 1961–1989* (New York: Harper Collins, 2007), p. xix.
11. Tuohy, William. "Up to 1 Million Demand Reform in E. Germany." *Los Angeles Times*, November 5, 1989. http://articles.latimes.com/1989-11-05/news/mn-1607_1_east-germany
12. Ibid.
13. Nepstad, p. 50.
14. Taylor, p. 428.

Chapter 5. A Continuing Struggle

1. Witte, Griff. "Tahrir Square Remains Primary Battle Site in Duel for Egypt's Future." *Washington Post*, February 4, 2011. http://www.washingtonpost.com/wp-dyn/content/article/2011/02/04/AR2011020401388.html
2. "Timeline: Egypt's Revolution." Aljazeera, February 14, 2011. www.aljazeera.com/news/middleeast/2011/01/201112515334871490.html
3. Robins, Philip. *The Middle East* (London: Oneworld Publications, 2016), p. 217.
4. Ibid., p. 218.
5. Shehadeh, Raja, and Penny Johnson (eds). *Shifting Sands* (Northampton, MA: Olive Branch Press, 2016), p. 70.
6. "Timeline: Egypt's Revolution."
7. Robins, p. 218.
8. "Timeline: Egypt's Revolution."

Works Consulted

Abdulhamid, Ammar. "Why Nonviolence Failed in Syria." *Now*, March 19, 2013. https://now.mmedia.me/lb/en/commentaryanalysis/why-nonviolence-failed-in-syria

Al-Jazeera. "Timeline: Egypt's Revolution." *Al-jazeera*, February 14 2011. www.aljazeera.com/news/middleeast/2011/01/201112515334871490.html

Baker, Mark Allen. *Spies of Revolutionary Connecticut: From Benedict Arnold to Nathan Hale*. Stroud, UK: The History Press, 2014.

BBC News. "South Korea's presidential scandal." BBC, May 9 2017. http://www.bbc.com/news/world-asia-37971085

Beard, Mary. *SPQR*. New York: Liveright Publishing, 2015.

Boston Tea Party Ship & Museum. www.bostonteapartyship.com/tea-blog/boston-tea-party

CNN Library. "Tiananmen Square Fast Facts." CNN, June 3 2016. www.cnn.com/2013/09/15/world/asia/tiananmen-square-fast-facts

Dawson, James. "Why Britain Created Monarchies in the Middle East." *The New Statesman*, August 15, 2014. http://www.newstatesman.com/politics/2014/08/why-britain-created-monarchies-

middle-east

Dwyer, Colin. "Venezuela Erupts In 'Mother of All Protests' As Anti-Maduro Sentiment Seethes." NPR, April 19 2017. http://www.npr.org/sections/thetwo-way/2017/04/19/524708302/venezuela-erupts-in-mother-of-all-protests-as-anti-maduro-sentiment-seethes

Ferling, John. *Independence: The Struggle to Set America Free*. New York: Bloomsbury Press, 2011.

Gandhi, Mohandas K. *Gandhi An Autobiography: The Story of My Experiments with Truth*. Boston: Beacon Press, 1993.

Gilder-Lehrman Institute of American History. "The Stamp Act, 1765." www.gilderlehrman.org/history-by-era/road-revolution/resources/stamp-act-1765

Godlewski, Nina. "John Adams Renounced Tea for Coffee in 1774." Boston.com, September 29 2015. www.boston.com/news/local-news/2015/09/29/john-adams-renounced-tea-for-coffee-in-1774

History.com staff. "Salt March." History.com, 2010. www.history.com/topics/salt-march

History.com staff. "The Boston Tea Party." History.com, 2009. www.history.com/topics/american-revolution/boston-tea-party

Holland, Ben. *Flashpoints in History*. New York: Octopus Publishing Group, 2016.

Jian, Ma. "The Great Tiananmen Taboo." *The Guardian*, June 1 2009. https://www.theguardian.com/world/2009/jun/02/tiananmen-square-protests-1989-china

Kaiman, Jonathan. "Hong Kong's Umbrella Revolution—The Guardian Briefing." *The Guardian*, September 30 2014. https://www.theguardian.com/world/2014/sep/30/-sp-hong-kong-umbrella-revolution-pro-democracy-protests

Kowalczyk, Henryk A. "Capitalism, Socialism and Communism." *Huffington Post*, November 10, 2016. http://www.huffingtonpost.com/henryk-a-kowalczyk/capitalism-socialism-and-_b_8523486.html

Lim, Louisa. *The People's Republic of Amnesia: Tiananmen Revisited*. Oxford: Oxford University Press, 2015.

"Luc Besson: Guardian interviews at the BFI." *The Guardian*, March 23 2000. www.theguardian.com/film/2000/mar/23/guardianinterviewsatbfisouthbank1

Madawi al-Rasheed. "Kuwaiti Activists Targeted under GCC Security Pact." *Al-Monitor,* March 2015. http://www.al-monitor.com/pulse/originals/2015/03/saudi-gcc-security-dissident-activism-detention-opposition.html

McGeown, Kate. "People Power at 25: Long road to Philippine Democracy." BBC News, February 25 2011. www.bbc.com/news/world-asia-pacific-12567320

Nepstad, Sharon Erickson. *Nonviolent Revolutions: Civil Resistance in the Late 20th Century*. Oxford: Oxford University Press, 2011.

North, Michael. *The Baltic*. Cambridge, MA: Harvard University Press, 2016.

Obama, Barack. "Remarks by President Obama to the People of Estonia." The White House Office of the Press Secretary, September 3 2014. https://obamawhitehouse.archives.gov/the-press-office/2014/09/03/remarks-president-obama-people-estonia.

Rayman, Noah. "6 Things You Should Know About the Tiananmen Square Massacre." *Time* magazine, May 19 2016. www.time.com/2822290/tiananmen-square-massacre-facts-time

Reyes-Estrope, Carmela. "Radyo Veritas Role in EDSA I Recalled." *Inquirer Northern Luzon*, February 25 2015 http://newsinfo.inquirer.net/675077/veritas-role-in-edsa-i-recalled

Robins, Philip. *The Middle East*. London: Oneworld Publications, 2016.

Rosenberg, Tina. "How to Topple a Dictatorship." *The New York Times*, February 13, 2015. https://opinionator.blogs.nytimes.com/2015/02/13/a-military-manual-for-nonviolent-war/?_r=0

Schirmer, Daniel B. and Stephen R. Shalom, (eds). *The Philippines Reader: A History of Colonialism, Neocolonialism, Dictatorship, and Resistance*. New York: South End Press, 1999.

Shehadeh, Raja and Penny Johnson, (eds). *Shifting Sands*. Northampton, MA: Olive Branch Press, 2016.

Starr, John Bryan. *Understanding China: A Guide to China's Economy, History, and Political Culture*. New York: Hill and Wang, 2010.

Stephan, Maria J. "Why Support for Syria's Nonviolent Fighters Is Key to Ending the War." *Common Dreams*, April 23, 2017. https://www.commondreams.org/views/2017/04/23/why-support-syrias-nonviolent-fighters-key-ending-war

Taylor, Frederick. *The Berlin Wall: A World Divided*, 1961–1989. New York: Harper Collins, 2007.

Tuohy, William. "Up to 1 Million Demand Reform in E. Germany: East Bloc: Demonstrators Seek Free Elections, End to Communist Domination. It's Nation's Biggest Protest." *Los Angeles Times*, November 5 1989. http://articles.latimes.com/1989-11-05/news/mn-1607_1_east-germany Yom, Sean. "How Middle Eastern Monarchies Survived the Arab Spring." *The Washington Post*, July 29, 2016. https://www.washingtonpost.com/news/monkey-cage/wp/2016/07/29/the-emerging-monarchies-club-in-the-middle-east/

Vila, Alexandra Caole. "29 interesting Facts About the EDSA Revolution." *The Philippine Star*, February 25 2015. www.philstar.com/news-feature/2015/02/25/1425819/29-interesting-facts-about-edsa-revolution

Witte, Griff. "Tahrir Square Remains Primary Battle Site in Duel for Egypt's Future." *Washington Post*, February 4, 2011. www.washingtonpost.com/world/tahrir-square-remains-primary-battle-site-in-duel-for-egypts-future/2011/02/04/ABJlnxQ_story.html?utm_term=.7f0639b3a92d

Zunes, Stephen. "Estonia's Singing Revolution (1986–1991)." International Center on Nonviolent Conflict, April 2009. www.nonviolent-conflict.org/estonias-singing-revolution-1986-1991

GLOSSARY

anarchy (AN-ar-kee)—A state of lawlessness due to the lack of a government or authority.

Baltic (BAL-tik)—Relating to the countries of Lithuania, Estonia, and Latvia, or to the Baltic Sea.

benevolent (be-NEV-uh-lent)—Structured for the purpose of doing good deeds.

boycott (BOY-kot)—An organized refusal to deal with a person, group or government in order to demand a change

Communist (KOM-yoo-nist)—Belonging to a system of government that seeks the elimination of private property in favor of commonly shared possessions.

defection (dee-FEK-shen)—To abandon or leave a cause or loyalty.

dictator (DIK-tay-ter)—A person in charge of a government who has unlimited and often oppressive power.

Forum (FOR-um)—The public place at the center of ancient Rome where economic and governmental business took place.

fraudulent (FROD-joo-lent)—Something done with a dishonest intent.

hunger strike (HUN-ger STRYK) – a refusal to eat enough to live in order to force a change in law or policy.

impeach (im-PEECH)—To force an elected official to leave office, often for misconduct.

imperialism (im-PEER-ee-uh-li-zem)—A nation's policy to extend its power beyond its borders to directly or indirectly control the affairs of other countries.

impoverishing (im-PAH-vrish-ing)—Making poorer.

martial law (MAR-shel LAW)—Using the military to limit freedoms during an occupation or in an emergency.

pastoral (pas-TOR-ral)—Related to the spiritual guidance of a church's congregation.

rebellious (ree-BEL-yes)—Intending to disobey or actively fight against authority

repressive (ree-PRES-iv)—Intending to prevent expression, free movement, dissenting opinions and other freedoms.

reunified (ree-YOO-neh-fyd)—Brought back together after being separated.

secession (sih-SEH-shen)—To officially withdraw from an organization or nation.

tribune (TRIH-byoon)—An official in ancient Rome who defended the poorer citizens from the rich and powerful.